JUL - 2019

U.S. AIR FORCE

by Jill Sherman

AMICUS | AMICUS INK

Amicus High Interest is published by Amicus and Amicus Ink
P.O. Box 1329, Mankato, MN 56002
www.amicuspublishing.us

Library of Congress Cataloging-in-Publication Data
Names: Sherman, Jill, author.
Title: U.S. Air Force / by Jill Sherman.
Description: Mankato, Minnesota : Amicus, [2019] | Series: Serving our
 country | Includes index. | Audience: Grades K-3.
Identifiers: LCCN 2018002158 | ISBN 9781681515601 (library binding) |
ISBN 9781681515984 (ebook) | ISBN 9781681523989 (pbk.)
Subjects: LCSH: United States. Air Force--Juvenile literature.
Classification: LCC UG633 .S455 2018 | DDC 358.400973--dc23
LC record available at https://lccn.loc.gov/2018002158

Photo Credits: DVIDS/U.S. Air Force photo by Staff Sgt. Joe W. McFadden/
Released cover; Shutterstock/Nikola m background pattern; Alamy/
IS098QB9U 2; Flickr/U.S. Air Force photo by Staff Sgt. Jacob N. Bailey 4–5;
DVIDS/U.S. Air Force photo by Staff Sgt. Shawn Nickel 6; DVIDS/U.S. Air
Force Photo by Airman 1st Class Jackson N. Haddon 9; DVIDS/U.S. Air
Force photo by Staff Sgt. Katrina Brisbin 10–11; Getty/Erik Simonsen 13;
WikiCommons/Master Sgt. Andy Dunaway by U.S. Air Force 14–15; Getty/
Tyler Stableford 17; Getty/Erik Simonsen 19; DVIDS/
TSgt Nic Kuetemeyer 20; iStock/kojihirano 22

Editor: Wendy Dieker
Designer: Aubrey Harper
Photo Researcher: Holly Young

Printed in China

HC 10 9 8 7 6 5 4 3 2 1
PB 10 9 8 7 6 5 4 3 2 1

TABLE OF CONTENTS

MIGHTY FLYERS

Are you ready to take off? The U.S.
Air Force zips through the sky. In
fighter jets and cargo planes, the
Air Force keeps our country safe.
They even defend us from space!

FLYING HIGH

The men and women of the Air Force are called airmen. Many airmen fly planes. The pilot sits in the **cockpit**. The copilot helps fly the plane. A **navigator** might join the crew.

Force Fact

Airmen can have many different jobs. Some are doctors. Some fix planes. Others fight fires.

EYE IN THE SKY

No plane is alone in the sky. Pilots always have help from the ground. Air traffic controllers use **radar** to see where the planes are. They chart a safe path for the pilots.

Force Fact
The Air Force flies the president's plane. Air traffic controllers call his plane "Air Force One."

AIR DROP

Disaster strikes. People on an island need supplies right away. The Air Force loads planes with food and water. There is not enough room to land on the beach. But that's ok. They push crates from the plane. The goods **parachute** safely to the ground.

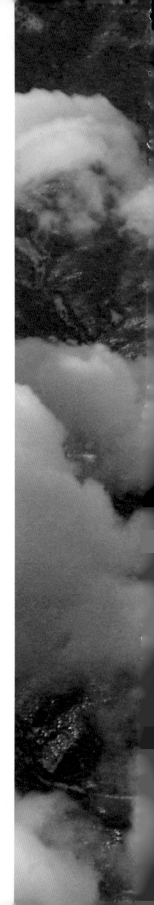

DRONES

Who is hiding in enemy lands? The Air Force can find out. They send a **drone**. The pilot can safely fly the drone from the ground. The drone sends back photos. It spotted an enemy base!

RIGHT ON TARGET

An enemy's base is found. The Air Force sends the B-1 bomber. The crew flies over the **target**. They drop a bomb. It's a hit! The enemy base is destroyed.

FIGHTER JETS

Air Force fighter jets are always ready to defend the country. An enemy plane attacks a U.S. army base. The F-15E Strike Eagle takes off. It fights back. It is the fastest fighter jet.

Force Fact
A pilot who has shot down five or more enemy planes is called an "ace."

SPACE COMMAND

The Air Force uses **satellites**. They watch the world's airspace. An enemy might fire a missile. The Air Force sends a missile at it. It will take out the enemy missile before anyone is hurt.

SKY FIGHTERS

The fast fighting machines of the Air Force are ready for takeoff. Equipped with guns and bombs, they are ready to attack. They zip through our skies. They swoop and dive. Every day, the brave men and women of the Air Force keep us safe.

U.S. AIR FORCE FAST FACTS

Founded: 1947

Members called: Airmen

Main duties: To protect and defend the nation from the air and space

Members on active duty: 315,000

Motto: "Integrity first, Service before self, Excellence in all we do."

WORDS TO KNOW

cockpit The place in an aircraft for the pilot and crew to sit and control the aircraft.

drone An unmanned aircraft that is controlled from the ground; drones can be programmed to operate by themselves too.

navigator The person in an aircraft crew who uses maps and instruments to direct the pilot's journey.

parachute To drop from an aircraft with a parachute; a parachute is a big piece of light fabric that opens up like a balloon to make an object fall more slowly.

radar A device that detects objects, such as aircraft, using radio waves.

satellite A machine that orbits Earth; it sends information and photos to the ground.

target A person, object, or place picked out for an attack.

LEARN MORE

Books

Boothroyd, Jennifer. *Inside the US Air Force*. Minneapolis: Lerner Books, 2017.

Doden, Matthew. *The US Air Force*. Mankato, Minn.: Capstone Publishers, 2017.

Marx, Mandy. *Amazing US Air Force Facts*. Mankato, Minn.: Capstone Publishers, 2017.

Websites

National Museum of the Air Force
www.nationalmuseum.af.mil

Official Home Page of the US Air Force
www.af.mil

INDEX